Inspiring Words
FROM THE PSALMS

Blue Sky Ink
Brentwood, Tennessee

It is you who light my lamp;
the LORD, my God, lights up my darkness.

Psalm 18:28 NRSV

Contents

Introduction

The book of Psalms represents the voices of those who explore the spiritual dimensions of life. It is the prayer book for those who want to know God's presence every day. The book of Psalms looms

as a tall sentinel on a high hill, inviting you to faith and courage.

In 1977, Anatoly Shcharansky was arrested for his attempt to emigrate from the Soviet Union to Israel. He spent thirteen years in prison and studied all one hundred and fifty psalms every day. His wife said that "in a lonely cell, locked alone with the book of Psalms, my husband found expression for his innermost feelings in the outpourings of the King of Israel, who lived thousands of years ago."

As you meditate on words from the Psalms, you can hear yourself speak to God and God speak to you. In that conversation, God's presence and your peace are known and cherished.

Blessed be the Lord, for he has heard the sound of my pleadings. The LORD is my strength and my shield; in him my heart trusts; so I am helped, and my heart exults, and with my song I give thanks to him.

PSALM 28:6–7 NRSV

A Strong Tower

You are my refuge, a high tower where my enemies
can never reach me.
PSALM 61:3 TLB

A storm suddenly strikes the shoreline. Men, women, and children, old and young, run for cover. Huge waves pound the sand. Gulls caw, boats are tossed to and fro as shipmates try to control their crafts. Birds scatter. Umbrellas collapse. Paper plates and beach blankets are carried off in the wind. Lifeguards scan the sea from their high tower, looking for swimmers who may be caught in the surf.

When you are pounded by the storms of life, it's tempting to take matters into your own hands—to quit a job, to leave a relationship, to cut yourself off from God's love and direction, to stand alone without protection. Such moves usually end in more pain than you started with. But there is another way. You can take refuge in the high tower that is God himself.

As the wind howls and the rain pelts your health,
your job, your relationships, run to God—first. He
is there, and his shelter is everlasting.

The LORD is a refuge
for the oppressed, a
stronghold in times of
trouble. Those who
know your name will
trust in you, for you,
LORD, have never
forsaken those who
seek you.

PSALM 9:9–10 NIV

A Peak Experience

In you I trust, O my God.
Do not let me be put to shame,
nor let my enemies triumph over me.

PSALM 25:2 NIV

All for one. One for all. Two men and two women set out to reach the summit of Mount Whitney, the highest peak in the continental United States. They've been preparing for this moment for months, jogging up and down hills and trails to get their bodies in shape for the high elevation and planning how to do it. But no matter how carefully they organize their journey, they cannot control every detail. They know they must walk in trust.

Life in the valley is a lot like the trail to the mountaintop—full of twists and turns and unexpected pitfalls. You may find yourself carrying burdens that slow you down and keep you from reaching the heights God has for you. But you can change that course today by lifting your eyes to the Lord and trusting him in all things and in all ways.

Plan your steps, but trust God to direct them
according to his purpose. Only he knows the plans
he has for you——plans for hope and for a future.

Open up before GOD, keep
nothing back; he'll do
whatever needs to be done.

PSALM 37:5 THE MESSAGE

An Unforgettable Gift

*Blessed is he who considers the poor;
the LORD will deliver him in time of trouble.*
PSALM 41:1 NKJV

The cold wind whistled through the cracks in the small, wood-frame house in eastern Kentucky and snapped at Sam's legs. The boy

wanted to surprise his mother and sisters this Christmas morning with hot tea and toast with jam. Rations and money were short since his papa had died six months before. And the coal was almost gone. "God, what are we going to do?" Sam pleaded as he filled the kettle.

Suddenly a clatter in the backyard caught his attention. Two men were dumping coal into the coal bin. Sam ran out to stop them. He was certain they had the wrong house.

"No mistake," said the driver when Sam protested. "I got the address right here on this paper. It's a gift, son, though I swore I wouldn't tell who it's from. Be thankful and don't ask no more questions," the man said.

*When you think you're out of options, listen and
watch. God may have an unexpected gift for you,
too. His kindness cannot be matched.*

[Good people] will
always be remembered
and greatly praised,
because they were
kind and freely gave
to the poor.

PSALM 112:9 CEV

A Cry for Help

*Each morning I will look to you in heaven and lay
my requests before you, praying earnestly.*

PSALM 5:3 TLB

"Help! Somebody, help me." A huge piece of lumber had fallen and pinned a construction worker against a wall. His coworkers rushed to his side to move the board and free the crewman. Medics were called, and treated him on the spot for what turned out to be only minor cuts and bruises.

Are you a person who takes pride in meeting your own needs and solving your problems without asking for help? It's good to be a responsible person, but there may come a time when you are pinned to the wall of life through no fault of your own: a terminal illness, separation from a loved one, the loss of a job. And you may not be able to resolve the situation through your own power. Only God can help you then. The Bible teaches that when God's people cry out to him, he is quick to respond.

*God knows the sound of your voice, and he
welcomes your call for the help that only he can
provide.*

Make haste to help me,
O Lord, my salvation.

PSALM 38:22 KJV

Simple Pleasures

They who dwell in the ends of the earth
stand in awe of Your signs; You make the
dawn and the sunset shout for joy.

PSALM 65:8 NASB

"Come quick," Frank called to his wife, Kathryn.

"I'm too tired to be quick about anything," she teased, then strolled over to where her husband stood next to the tall pine in the front yard of their mountain cabin.

"Look at that sunset," he said, drawing her close. "I didn't want the day to end without you at my side to enjoy it."

Kathryn took a deep breath and felt her body relax against her husband after a long afternoon of yard work. As she looked at the golden sun slipping behind the distant hill, she was suddenly aware of a deep sense of joy and appreciation for the simple pleasures of God's creation.

The song of a bird winging overhead, the warmth of sunshine, the shade of a tree, and the fragrance of a flower can all restore inner peace and rekindle joy.

God created the heavens and the earth for his people
to enjoy and cherish, and to share with others.

Let all the joys of the godly
well up in praise to the Lord,
for it is right to praise him.

PSALM 33:1 TLB

In the Nick of Time

I will instruct you and teach you in the way you
should go; I will counsel you and watch over you.

PSALM 32:8 NIV

Eve couldn't understand why God told her not to eat of a certain tree in the Garden of Eden. Abraham couldn't understand why God asked him to sacrifice his son Isaac. Mary and Martha couldn't understand why God allowed their brother Lazarus to die without Jesus' intervening.

Maybe you don't understand why God has not healed your illness, restored your relationship with your parents, led you to the career you prepared for, showed you the way out of a financial bind, or sent you a spouse with whom to share your life. Plans and purposes that seem "right" to you may be stopped before you can complete them. Relationships that appear supportive and wholesome evaporate. You may feel that everything you touch turns to dust.

God says it is not necessary for his people to know
and to understand. It is enough to be assured that
the Master has a plan and that you are included.
You can rest in that certainty.

Show me your paths
and teach me to follow.

PSALM 25:4 CEV

A Friendship Repaired

Though sins fill our hearts, you forgive them all.
PSALM 65:3 TLB

"Did you see Paulette?" Jan's friend Rita whispered.

Of course Jan saw her. How could she miss Paulette, standing there making a fashion statement, as always. Jan turned to avoid facing her former friend—the one who had betrayed her confidence when she most needed someone to lean on.

Suddenly Paulette was next to her, out of breath and teary-eyed. "Jan," she stammered, "I know things ended badly between us. I want you to know I'm truly sorry for what I did. Will you forgive me?"

Jan caught her breath. Her own eyes were now wet. "Yes," she whispered, choking with emotion as God's Spirit prompted her to admit her wrong as well. "And will you forgive me for hating you all these years?" The two reached for each other and, in an instant of grace, forgave the hurts that had kept them apart.

Everyone causes hurt. No one is exempt. But you will feel joy when you acknowledge what you've done and ask for forgiveness.

If You, LORD, should mark iniquities,
O Lord, who could stand?
But there is forgiveness with You,
that You may be feared.

PSALM 130:3–4 NASB

The Best Stew

*I thought about the wrong direction in which I was
headed, and turned around and came running back to you.*

PSALM 119:60 TLB

Rachel arrived in Central Africa, eager to do something big for
God, even though she knew the missions trip would be a challenge.
The first night she looked forward to running the projector for a film about the life of
Jesus. But she was assigned the evening meal
instead.

Rachel was upset. She hadn't come
across the globe to make stew. She had come
to make a difference for Jesus. But as she
chopped the meat and cut up carrots and
potatoes, two children ran up to her, each
holding up a small bowl. Behind them, a line of mothers with babies
and toddlers began to form. Tears ran down her face. *I almost
missed this opportunity*, thought Rachel, *because I have been so
focused on what I wanted to do rather than on what God wanted
for me—to serve where I was needed most.*

*God teaches that his way is ultimately the best
way—even when people resist learning this
important truth. Then he turns their resistance
into praise.*

Come, everyone, and clap your hands for joy!
Shout to God with joyful praise!

PSALM 47:1 NLT

Ice Cream for Dessert

*We are the people of His Pasture
and the sheep of His hand.*
PSALM 95:7 NASB

Teresa and her husband, Don, noticed a caregiver had moved in to assist their elderly neighbor, Abby Johnson. They decided to invite the two for dinner, but that evening Abby was having a particularly bad time. Don seemed to know just what to do. He didn't try to reason with her. Don knew that ice cream was her favorite dessert. He said simply, "Abby, I have just the ticket—a bowl of strawberry ice cream. How does that sound? It always works for me when I'm upset about something." Abby's face lit up. All of a sudden she appeared to forget her complaints. She picked up her spoon, ready to start eating the moment Don served her.

Do you push God away or welcome him when you feel upset? He'll comfort, love, and care for you as his beloved child—if you let him. God knows what you need—even when you're not sure. You can always go to him and receive the care that only he can give.

O LORD, what are humans that you
should care about them?
What are mere mortals that you
should think about them?

PSALM 144:3 GOD'S WORD

Harry's Gift

Let the godly rejoice.
Let them be glad in God's presence.
Let them be filled with joy.

PSALM 68:3 NLT

"I'm so excited," Harry exclaimed to his cousin Richard, who was sitting on the edge of the hospital bed where Harry lay dying.

"About what?" Richard was incredulous. *What could be exciting to a man dying of liver cancer?* he wondered.

"Just think," Harry continued, "in a day or two, my pain will be gone and I'll be in heaven."

When Harry had been diagnosed with cancer two months before, he had talked more about going to heaven than about dying—even though he had been given only a few weeks to live. Richard squeezed his hand. "I'm excited for you, too," he choked.

That night Richard reflected on what had occurred in the hospital room. He thought about how he had been living his life—pretty much for himself—and decided that he wanted to give more of himself to others.

It is exciting to anticipate being with God forever
in heaven, and it is a joy to prepare for that day.

Restore to me again the joy
of your salvation, and make
me willing to obey you.
Then I will teach your
ways to other sinners.

PSALM 51:12–13 TLB

Blessings in a Box

O Lord my God, I will give thanks to You forever.
Psalm 30:12 NASB

The speaker stood before a group of men and women and held up a small decorated box. On one side, colorful letters spelled out

Blessing Box. Then she removed the lid and pulled out small squares of paper, each one a thank-you for a blessing received.

"Thank you, God, for a sunny day," she read aloud. "Thank you, God, for our new baby." "Thank you, God, for opening my eyes to the poor." "Thank you, God, for standing by me during the interview."

She encouraged the audience to make blessing boxes of their own, as a way to develop the habit of giving thanks each day. "Nothing is too serious or too silly to include," she said.

"Once a month, open the box and read the blessings," she suggested. "You will never be the same again in the face of God's great gifts."

The blessing box can be a powerful reminder to pause, notice God's many blessings, and give thanks for them.

*W*e give thanks to you,
O God; we give thanks.
You are present, and your
miracles confirm that.

PSALM 75:1 GOD'S WORD

A Soldier in Need

*I am constantly aware of your unfailing love, and I
have lived according to your truth.*

PSALM 26:3 NLT

During the Civil War, a man's only son joined the Union army. It broke the father's heart to say good-bye. He wondered if he'd ever  see his son again. One day a young soldier in a tattered uniform appeared at the bank and asked for help. The older man told him he was busy with customers, and referred him to the army headquarters.

The soldier then unfolded a soiled note and passed it to the banker, who read it aloud. "Father, this is one of my comrades, wounded in the last battle. Please take him in as you would me. Your loving son, Charlie." Suddenly everything changed. The banker embraced the young man and whisked him off to his spacious home, where he was cared for until he was well.

*God the Father, even more than an earthly father,
welcomes and helps anyone who comes to him and
asks. God provides what you need when you need
it. His love and protection are everlasting.*

The LORD opens the eyes of the blind;
the LORD raises those who are bowed down;
the LORD loves the righteous.

PSALM 146:8 NKJV

Peaceful Mealtimes

The tender grass grows up at his command to feed the cattle, and there are fruit trees, vegetables and grain for man to cultivate, and wine to make him glad . . . and bread to give him strength.

PSALM 104:14–15 TLB

"Happy Birthday, dear Grandma, happy birthday to you!" The family finished singing, prayed a blessing over the meal, then ushered Grandma to the seat at the head of the table and served her dinner on the special plate reserved for such occasions. In the Old Testament, people did something similar. They celebrated holy days, the harvest, wedding feasts, and other occasions, perhaps birthdays, too, with food and drink and prayer.

Peace and harmony around the table—whether at a party or in a small family setting—aid both digestion and disposition. You can achieve this by setting a lovely table and preparing and serving foods that family members particularly enjoy. Brother Lawrence, a Carmelite monk in the 1600s, turned his duties surrounding mealtimes into a humble prayer: "Lord of all pots and pans and things . . . make me a saint by getting meals and washing up the plates."

By inviting God to the dinner table through prayer, you'll be more aware of his bountiful provision.

They all wait for You
to give them their food in due season.
You give to them, they gather it up;
You open Your hand, they are satisfied with good.

Psalm 104:27–28 NASB

Dream House

God, make a fresh start in me, shape a
Genesis week from the chaos of my life.
PSALM 51:10 THE MESSAGE

lease, can we buy this house? Take my allowance for the whole year to help pay for it." Keith and Carol chuckled as their daughter Julie begged them to buy the white Cape Cod with the green trim.

"We'll see, honey. We like it too. Mom and I will pray about it and decide in the next day or two," Keith said. Keith and Carol spent the evening going over figures, floor plans, and decorating ideas. The house was sturdy, but it needed a lot of work inside before the family could move in. It looked good on the outside, but it needed some sprucing up on the inside before it could be their dream house.

ust as it takes time, money, and commitment to fix
up a house, it takes time, prayer, and commitment
to refurbish a life. God is more interested in how
you look on the inside than how you appear on the
outside. He will cleanse and rebuild the rooms of
your heart if you ask him.

Hear my prayer, O LORD,
and let my cry come to You.

PSALM 102:1 NKJV

Clutter's Last Stand

Give me understanding, and I shall keep Your law;
indeed, I shall observe it with my whole heart.
PSALM 119:34 NKJV

A Shaker hymn reminds listeners of an ancient truth: " 'Tis a gift to be simple." What a challenge, however, to put this sage advice into practice in an era of acquisition and consumption. Closets bulge with unused clothing, books, and rusty kitchenware. Old folders and yellowing paper clog file cabinets. Garages house gardening tools, bikes, and broken toys instead of cars.

But there is joy in a life free of pretense and clutter. Simplicity puts the things of the world in proper perspective. How liberating it could be to use something without owning it, to be free of dusting items you don't need, fixing things that continue to break, and replacing equipment that wears out.

How blessed you might feel to come down to where
you ought to be so God can lift you up to where he
wants you to be—in harmony with him. Every day
is an opportunity to reconnect with a simpler way
of life—giving away things you no longer need or,
sometimes, even something you treasure.

The law of the LORD is perfect,
reviving the soul. The statutes of
the LORD are trustworthy,
making wise the simple.

PSALM 19:7 NIV

Good-Bye, Dad

*You light my lamp; the LORD my God illumines
my darkness. For by You I can run upon a troop;
and by my God I can leap over a wall.*
PSALM 18:28–29 NASB

"Dad's in a coma." As Maureen listened to her brother, George, over the phone, she realized the long vigil at their father's side was nearly over. Moments later, she hurried into her dad's hospital room and took his frail hands in hers. She was filled with memories as she looked at the man she loved. He had always been a devoted father, and she had grown up knowing how much she was loved.

"Dear God, release him," she prayed. "I give him back to you." Maureen gently stroked his face. "Dad, I came to say good-bye and to thank you," she whispered. "George is here too. It's okay to let go. We love you." Later that afternoon, Maureen watched her father take one more ragged breath. Then he was gone. The room was suddenly filled with God's peace. Maureen knew then everything would be all right.

*God brings light to darkness and strength to the weak.
He hears and answers your prayers in the midst of grief.*

I call upon you, for you
will answer me, O God;
incline your ear to me;
hear my words.

PSALM 17:6 ESV

Rejection Slip

You have probed my heart. You have confronted me at night. You have tested me like silver, but you found nothing wrong. I have determined that my mouth will not sin.
PSALM 17:3 GOD'S WORD

Carl stared at the announcement of the autograph party scheduled that afternoon. He still couldn't believe his good fortune. After ten years of writing, his first novel had been published—a story based on the life of his maternal grandfather. It had mystery, politics, and romance. He envisioned a movie deal and TV appearances. He was sure the store would be packed. In fact, he had slipped two pens into his pocket in case one ran dry.

At 4:00 sharp Carl sat down at the table piled high with books. An hour later, only ten people had stopped by. Only four, his mother and sister among them, had purchased a book. Carl took a deep breath and sat back. Then he smiled—he had published a book. *Thank you, God.*

God will never fail you. He cares about every part of your life. Look to him for the encouragement you deserve.

*S*et a guard over my mouth, O LORD;
keep watch over the door of my lips.

PSALM 141:3 NIV

Welcome Cake

*Your beauty and love chase after me every
day of my life. I'm back home in the house
of GOD for the rest of my life.*

PSALM 23:6 THE MESSAGE

Rita stepped into the yard of her new home. She envisioned a rose garden at the rear and perhaps a fruit tree. Rita looked forward to living in this quiet neighborhood where she hoped to make a real friend. Suddenly the side gate clicked open and in walked a smiling woman.

"I'm Marty Warren," the woman said, extending a hand. "I live in the yellow house across the street. Welcome to Brookhaven!" Rita introduced herself as Marty handed her a gift box. Inside was a small round cake with a fresh rose on top and the word *Welcome* spelled out in pink icing. "I hope we can be friends," added Marty. "I've been longing for someone my age to move in. And here you are—an answer to prayer," she said, smiling.

Rita smiled. "Thank you." Marty was an answer to her prayer, too.

*God knows your dreams and desires even before
you do. He delights in fulfilling them in unexpected
ways. No one can equal or outdo his goodness.*

*H*ow great is Your goodness, which You have stored up for those who fear You, which You have wrought for those who take refuge in You, before the sons of men!

PSALM 31:19 NASB

Life Savings

No wonder we are happy in the Lord! For we are trusting him. We trust his holy name. Yes, Lord, let your constant love surround us, for our hopes are in you alone.

PSALM 33:21–22 TLB

"I need to stop by the bank," Raymond told his wife, Eileen, as he came in from the garden, his clothes soaked with perspiration and his hands black with dirt.

"What you need is a hot bath," she said, smiling. "The bank can wait till tomorrow."

Raymond took Eileen's advice and soaked himself clean, then sat down and snoozed. The next morning, however, the banks closed—for good. It was Black Tuesday, March 6, 1933. Raymond and millions more lost their life savings. Later that day, Raymond ran into his friend Lester and told him what happened. On the spot, Lester reached into his pocket and pulled out $900. "It's all I have in the world," he said, "but you have nothing. Here, half is yours," said Lester as he handed Raymond $450 in bills.

When you are down to your last dollar or have reached the bottom emotionally, look up. God is there, waiting to restore you, to give you hope and a future.

May integrity and honesty protect me, for I put my hope in you.

PSALM 25:21 NLT

Yes to Life

You will not delight in sacrifice, or I would give it;
you will not be pleased with a burnt offering. The
sacrifices of God are a broken spirit; a broken and
contrite heart, O God, you will not despise.

PSALM 51:16–17 ESV

Life is difficult, complicated, multilayered, and unpredictable.

Even so, life is more satisfying and ultimately more joyful when you embrace it instead of resisting it. Some people call such behavior "going with the flow." Others see it as surrendering to God's plan.

Deborah, one of the judges in the Old Testament of the Bible, was such a person. She ruled Israel from under a tree known throughout the country as "the Palm of Deborah." As a judge and prophet, she was a vessel of God's will to the people at a time in history when most women were home cooking or weaving or caring for children. And when God called his people into battle, Deborah obeyed him too. She did not argue or try to outguess God. She said yes to the life he planned for her.

Life is the most satisfying when people express the
gifts and talents God gave them, when they are
humble in heart and say yes to his plans.

The fear of the LORD is the beginning of wisdom. Good sense is shown by everyone who follows God's guiding principles. His praise continues forever.

PSALM 111:10 GOD'S WORD

Desert Getaway

Lovingkindness and truth have met together;
righteousness and peace have kissed each other. Truth
springs from the earth, and righteousness looks down
from heaven. Indeed, the LORD will give what is good,

PSALM 85:10–12 NASB

Gordon lay under a blanket of stars in a tent with his grandson Gabe. Just after they had snuggled into their sleeping bags, they held

hands and thanked God for a wonderful day of hiking and rock scrambling.

"Grandpa," Gabe whispered in the darkness, "I wish we could stay here forever. It's so peaceful. At home I get tired of playing computer games and riding my bike. I'd never get tired of being here. I could climb those hills every day and never get bored."

Gabe said good night, then turned over and closed his eyes. Gordon smiled at his young grandson, who seemed to know what really mattered in life. "Good night, Gabe," he said.

Gorden and Gabe had come to the desert to get away and have fun. God refreshed them by displaying his splendor in the hills by day and in the stars at night.

Spending time in nature is a wonderful way to get refreshed
and to learn more about God through his beautiful creation.

I will open my mouth in parables,
I will utter hidden things, things from of old—
what we have heard and known,
what our fathers have told us.
We will not hide them from their children;
we will tell the next generation
the praiseworthy deeds of the LORD.

PSALM 78:2–4 NIV

The Best Kind of Love

*I will go about Your altar, O LORD, that I may proclaim
with the voice of thanksgiving, and tell of all Your
wondrous works. LORD, I have loved the habitation of
Your house, and the place where Your glory dwells.*

PSALM 26:6–8 NKJV

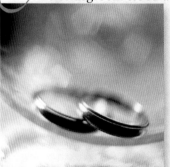

The bridegroom stood at the front of the church, waiting nervously for the doors at the back to open. The organist began to play the first notes of "Here Comes the Bride." Suddenly his bride was walking down the aisle, a vision of beauty and innocence in her white dress, her hair crowned with a wreath of fresh flowers.

His heart leaped at the sight of her—the woman to whom he was about to pledge his heart for as long as he lived. He reflected on their months together before this day, their desire to be one. Both of them had anticipated the joy of their wedding day and the fulfillment of their first night as husband and wife. God had brought them together, they were sure of that. And both of them had committed to God and to each other to remain pure until they spoke their wedding vows.

*God has a plan for marriage, and when that plan is
followed, blessings and honor flow freely.*

Reverence for the LORD is pure, lasting forever.
The laws of the LORD are true; each one is fair.

PSALM 19:9 NLT

The Test

O you who love the LORD, hate evil! He preserves the lives
of his saints; he delivers them from the hand of the wicked.

PSALM 97:10 ESV

When Rhonda walked into the department store, unsought memories flooded her mind. Years before, as a young teen, she had stolen something from this same store—a pair of earrings that she had tucked inside her bag. Rhonda was one of the lucky ones who had been caught, and she had made restitution and been forgiven. She vowed at the time never to shoplift again. She didn't like who she had become, and she wanted to live a clean life, to do what she knew was right.

Today as she walked past the counters in the jewelry department, she had no more temptation to shoplift the glittering baubles. God had removed that temptation in answer to her prayers, and in its place Rhonda had an abiding desire to thank and praise God.

People know in their hearts what is right and
wrong. God is ready to show mercy and grace to
anyone who wants to turn from wrong to right.

I confess my iniquity;
I am troubled by my sin.

PSALM 38:18 NIV

A Widow's Surprise

Gracious is the LORD, and righteous;
yes, our God is compassionate.

PSALM 116:5 NASB

A widow in Zarephath, a village near Sidon, Lebanon, was a victim of a terrible famine. She had nothing to plant or harvest, and she feared for herself and her son. The prophet Elijah came to her door and asked for shelter. Queen Jezebel was trying to kill him, and he needed refuge.

The woman had nothing to share. Her flour jar and oil jug were nearly empty. But Elijah knew that God would provide, and he told the woman not to worry. Her bottle of oil and jar of flour would not become empty before God sent rain on the dry land. Day after day the widow witnessed a miracle of provision. The jar and the jug were never full, but they were never empty either. Her heart softened, and she began trusting God to provide.

Even when your worst fears come true, you can
still trust God. His compassion cannot be equaled.
No one will care for you as God will.

The LORD will provide justice for his people and have compassion on his servants.

PSALM 135:14 GOD'S WORD

Heavenly Home

What you say goes, GOD, and stays,
as permanent as the heavens.
PSALM 119:89 THE MESSAGE

God says he has prepared a place in heaven for all who follow and believe in him. Some people think heaven is filled with palaces and streets paved with gold. Others envision choirs of angels sitting at the throne of God, praising his name in glorious song. Still others might wonder what you will do in heaven, and whether you will enjoy again the company of friends and family you knew on earth. And what about your dog or cat? Will Fido or Fluffy join you there?

These are big questions, and there are no firm answers this side of heaven. But one thing is certain, and that is the supreme authority and reign of God for all eternity. You can count on his love, his justice, and his promise of life to come, for all who follow him.

You don't need to fret or try to figure out what is
ahead. Trust God. He will not let you down.

The LORD is King for ever and ever; the nations will perish from his land.

PSALM 10:16 NIV

Battle Fatigue

Bless the Lord who is my immovable Rock. He gives me strength and skill in battle. He is always kind and loving to me; he is my fortress, my tower of strength and safety, my deliverer.

PSALM 144:1–2 TLB

Paul and Elizabeth met, fell in love, married, and in an instant became stepparents. Between them they had four daughters and two sons. Elizabeth was sure that, with God's help, her love for her husband and Paul's love for her would carry them through.

The task of dealing with so many personalities could have been overwhelming, but Elizabeth knew that God was at her side and would give her the wisdom and compassion she needed. Perhaps you face a similar situation. You may be a stepparent already or contemplating marrying someone with children. Take heart. God will equip you for the spiritual task as well as for the daily interactions, and he will see you through. He will use this experience to turn your heart to him and to the deep needs of the young people who deserve your love and care.

There is no situation too great for God. He will equip you, guide you, and give you the victory if you turn often to him in prayer.

You have armed me with
strength for the battle;
You have subdued under
me those who rose up
against me.

PSALM 18:39 NKJV

Count on Me

The LORD abides forever;
He has established His throne for judgment,
and he will judge the world in righteousness;
He will execute judgment for the peoples with equity.

PSALM 9:7–8 NASB

"There is no justice." You've probably heard this statement or said it yourself. You may have lost a potential job because a traffic tie-up prevented you from being on time. You may have lost your heart to someone who walked out on you. You may have worked hours on a project only to realize that you had been given the wrong information at the outset. A person you respected may have disappointed you by leading a double life.

Life on earth is filled with injustices. Since the Garden of Eden, human circumstances have been difficult. It is hard to contemplate that the God of the universe can forgive and love everyone—yet he does. And that is the saving grace by which you can live. Justice will prevail, and you can trust God for that.

No matter what is going on in life, God is in control.
You can't have a problem too big for him to resolve, and
you can't be too broken for him to pick up and restore.

The Right and Justice are the roots of your rule; Love and Truth are its fruits.

PSALM 89:14 THE MESSAGE

Just Say It

*Keep your tongue from evil and your lips from
speaking deceit. Turn away from evil and do
good; seek peace and pursue it.*

PSALM 34:13–14 ESV

The phone rang as Paula pulled the ice cream from the freezer.

"Hi, Paula. It's Carmen. Did I catch you at a bad time?"

"I have a few minutes," Paula said. But she was holding up her bridge group. "What's up?"

"I called to invite you to a jewelry party at my house next Saturday. I'm starting a home-based business, and I'm asking my friends to back me up. Can I count on you?"

"I'll check my calendar," Paula said. She needed to say no because she had promised herself not to book any more social engagements until after the first of the month. *Enough of the "polite" lies,* she thought. Then Paula blurted out the truth. Carmen was disappointed but not upset. Paula was grateful that she had finally told the truth. It really was better, and she promised herself to continue doing so from that point on.

*God blesses the person who turns away from
lying and commits to telling the truth.*

Blessed is the person whom the
LORD never accuses of sin and who
has no deceitful thoughts.

PSALM 32:2 GOD'S WORD

Shimmering Seashells

*The LORD is good to everyone and has compassion
for everything that he has made. Everything that
you have made will give thanks to you, O LORD,
and your faithful ones will praise you.*

PSALM 145:9–10 GOD'S WORD

"Auntie Lynn, come quick," Patty shouted, holding up a beautiful seashell. Lynn walked down the shoreline to where Patty was sitting on the sand. Her cup was already half full. She spread out the shells for her aunt to see. "Can I keep them?" she asked.

"Of course," Lynn replied. "First we'll wash them, and then we'll polish them with a soft cloth. I have a little jar you can use to carry them back home. What a lovely souvenir they'll be of our weekend together." Is your life a bit like a seashell, nice looking at quick glance, but truly radiant when you rinse away the grit that clings?

*It takes time to uncover the things that mask your
natural beauty, but God is there to help loosen
negative habits and actions so you can display all
the gifts he has given you. Washing away hurts,
habits, and unhealthy traits may take some doing,
but the result is a life that reflects the image of God.*

Sing to Him, sing praises to Him;
Speak of all His wonders.
Glory in His holy name;
Let the heart of those who seek
the LORD be glad.

PSALM 105:2–3 NASB

No Shame on Me

I have clung tightly to your written instructions.
O LORD, do not let me be put to shame. I will
eagerly pursue your commandments because you
continue to increase my understanding.

PSALM 119:31–32 GOD'S WORD

Shame can be a good thing when you need to make amends for a wrong action. But perhaps you feel shame for things over which you have no control or responsibility: a friend turns his back on you; your adult child makes a poor moral choice; your position at work is terminated; you didn't meet your sales quota; you make a simple mistake or make a clumsy move. Does your face turn red? Do you feel ashamed?

God says to hold up your head and walk in the light. He hears your shout for help when you need him, and your call for assistance when someone takes action against you. His grace and mercy are new every morning. There is no shame for those who follow his teaching and live in his light.

Healthy shame is important to a life of integrity, but
shame for no sound reason separates you from God.
Stay close to him, and you'll never hang your head again.

Those who look to him are radiant, and their faces shall never be ashamed.

PSALM 34:5 ESV

Promise Keeper

*The LORD is righteous in everything he does; he is
filled with kindness. The LORD is close to all who
call on him, yes, to all who call on him sincerely.*
PSALM 145:17–18 NLT

"I'll pay the bills tonight. I promise." "I promise I'll order the tickets this evening." "I'll have the quote to you before 5:00. It's a prom-

ise." People make and break promises
24/7. Imagine how the world would
change if men and women simply did
what they said they were going to do
when they said they'd do it. Make that
phone call. Write that letter. Pay that bill.
Visit that friend.

There is no one who has never broken a single promise except
God. And you need never be afraid that he will suddenly break a
promise made. He won't break a promise because he is the one who
created the universe and all that is within it. He will be there for you
no matter what. You can count on God.

*God is the one and only true keeper of promises.
What he says he will do, he does. He cannot go
back on his word, for it is true and right and just.*

$\mathscr{G}$OD always does what he says,
and is gracious in everything he does.

PSALM 145:13 THE MESSAGE

The Phone Call

The steps of a man are established by the LORD;
and He delights in his way. When he falls, he
will not be hurled headlong, because the LORD is
the One who holds his hand.

PSALM 37:23–24 NASB

Victoria whispered a silent prayer, then rehearsed one last time what she intended to say during the phone call she was about to make. Too much time had already passed, and she needed to talk to her father now. "Dad, I'm calling to tell you how much I love you. I've made some mistakes in relating to you, and I want to change right now for the better. I want to focus on what really matters—being together and enjoying whatever time we have. You mean so much to me."

Victoria breathed deeply, picked up the phone, and dialed the familiar number. When she heard her father's voice, God's peace flooded her heart. She couldn't even remember why she had waited so long, but she knew the time was right, and the words she planned to say were from her heart.

When you bring God into your decision-making process, you will be assured of perfect peace and a sound and wise decision.

Great peace have those who love Your law; and nothing causes them to stumble.

PSALM 119:165 NKJV

A Good Night's Sleep

I will lie down and sleep in peace, for you alone,
O LORD, make me dwell in safety.

PSALM 4:8 NIV

Everyone wants a good night's sleep, rest from the stress of daily living. Sleep is essential for balanced health, an alert mind, and a relaxed attitude. But for millions of people it's hard to come by. Sixty-hour-a-week jobs, children to care for, homes to maintain, and neighbors and friends to interact with, consume many of the hours that should be set aside for rest.

There is no need to pop a pill or count sheep. A growing number of men and women have found the answer in God's teaching. You can rest in God and then count your blessings. God says that when you lie down your sleep will be sweet, and you will awaken refreshed and restored, for he has watched over you all night long.

When you commit your day to God, then rest in him
at night, you are assured of the sleep you need, as
well as a new and fresh perspective the next morning.

I lay down and slept. I woke up in safety,
for the LORD was watching over me.

PSALM 3:5 NLT

Enough Light

*Send your light and your truth. Let them
guide me. Let them bring me to your holy
mountain and to your dwelling place.*

PSALM 43:3 GOD'S WORD

Art needed a break, so he rented a mountain cabin for a weekend. Art remembered how much he had loved the woods when he was a kid. He had even talked to God there, whenever he was afraid and when no one was looking.

"Lord," he prayed during a stroll one evening, "I'm up to my chin in work. And I'm stuck. Please, would you shed some light on this case? In fact," he said, chuckling, "I could use more light to get back to the cabin. This flashlight is a loser. I can't see but a step ahead." *H'm.* Art reflected on his own words. *Is God telling me something?* he wondered. *Maybe that's all I really need—enough light for the next step.* He smiled heavenward, then walked back to the cabin.

*There is no need to spend a lot of time and energy
trying to figure out what's next. God says all you
need is enough light for the next step.*

Even the darkness is not dark to you; the night is bright as the day, for darkness is as light with you.

PSALM 139:12 ESV

Shoeman Dan

He whose walk is blameless and who does what is righteous . . .
who does his neighbor no wrong and casts no slur on his
fellowman. . . He who does these things will never be shaken.

PSALM 15:2–5 NIV

It's easy to befriend people who are like you, but what about the ones who are different? Charles faced a challenge befriending Shoeman Dan, a deliberately disagreeable codger who used put-downs and sarcasm to interact with the other employees. Every morning, Dan greeted Charles with a jab. Charles would laugh it off and shoot back with a comment of his own. They carried on this way for months.

Then on Dan's seventieth birthday, Charles ordered a cake and rounded up the employees to sing "Happy Birthday." Dan was surprised when the staff burst into song. He said later that he had forgotten it was his birthday, that to him it was just another day. Six months later Dan died at home in bed. "I loved the guy," Charles said, choking back tears. "I didn't have to understand him. It wasn't hard. It never cost me a thing."

How easy it is to love the lovely. But God can
give you the grace to love the unlovely.

Light is sown for the righteous, and joy for the upright in heart. Rejoice in the LORD, O you righteous, and give thanks to his holy name!

PSALM 97:11–12 ESV

A New Song

*My heart is confident in you, O God; no wonder I can
sing your praises! Wake up, my soul! Wake up,
O harp and lyre! I will waken the dawn with my song.*

PSALM 57:7–8 NLT

Take your pick: classical, cool jazz, Americana, country-and-western, hip-hop, hard rock, metal, religious, inspirational—all kinds of music. Day and night you can sing, dance, gyrate, or just sit back and listen to your favorites. People can't get away from music—nor do they want to. Like love, it's a universal language.

Music soothes the soul, sparks creativity, and helps people access their deepest feelings that words sometimes cannot express. Music is the way many people worship heroes and honor celebrities. But God alone is the biggest celebrity in all of history. It's time for men, women, and children to up the ante—to worship God night and day, to stomp feet, strum guitars, pound keyboards, blow horns, lift hands, sing and dance with joy and in gratitude.

*From earliest times, music has been a means of
expressing one's deepest feelings. What better
way to express your feelings for God than by
making music with all you've got.*

I'm singing at the top of my lungs,
I'm so full of answered prayers.

PSALM 13:6 THE MESSAGE

Get Well Soon

*The LORD protects him and keeps him alive; he is
called blessed in the land; you do not give him up to
the will of his enemies. The LORD sustains him on his
sickbed; in his illness you restore him to full health.*

PSALM 41:2–3 ESV

How consoling it is to open a get-well note from a friend wishing
you a quick recovery from surgery or illness,
to hear that you're missed, that people are
pulling for you with prayer and warm wishes.
The words of encouragement can inspire you
to focus on getting well.

Good health is one of God's great blessings. And when you're down—as all human
beings are from time to time—he is there sus-
taining you, comforting you, and inspiring your health practitioners
to provide what you need. How have you been treating yourself? Are
you overworking? Asking your body to perform on only a few hours'
sleep? Expecting top performance without eating what you need?

*God will help you take the steps that will make the
difference between vibrant health and frequent
illness. With his direction you can begin a new season
today. Your body, mind, and spirit are gifts from
God. It makes sense to talk to the Great Physician
about how to maintain them for optimal well-being.*

God is my helper. The Lord is
the one who keeps me alive!

PSALM 54:4 NLT

Bob's Choice

Let your mercy comfort me as you promised. Let
your compassion reach me so that I may live,
because your teachings make me happy.
PSALM 119:76–77 GOD'S WORD

ob fingered the folded paper, an invitation to the Van Huesen
third annual family reunion. He hadn't been to one yet, and he didn't

plan to go to this one either. It was too
painful to be with Jenny's extended
family since she died. He hoped they
understood that without his wife, he
felt nothing was worth the effort.

Later that day the phone rang.
There was no mistaking the voice. It
was Jenny's brother Rich, who wanted him to attend. "We all miss
Jenny," he said, "but we all miss you, too. There are nieces and
nephews and new grandkids who want to get to know you. It won't
be the same without you." Bob cleared his throat and wiped his eyes,
then managed to whisper, "Thanks, Rich. I'll be there. You can
count on it."

God will comfort you and supply all your needs
even during the most difficult seasons of life.
Count on him, and he will not fail you.

*Y*ou will increase my
honor and comfort
me once again.

PSALM 71:21 NIV

The Best Defense

Stay with GOD! Take heart. Don't quit.
I'll say it again: Stay with GOD.
PSALM 27:14 THE MESSAGE

Sweetheart, I'm so discouraged. Let's cancel the newspaper," Lucille said to her husband across the breakfast table. "I'm so tired of all the disheartening news." She put the folded paper next to him.

"I don't like reading this stuff either," he said. "But we can't hide from the world we live in," he added. "Prayer is the best defense we have. I have an idea—let's pick out one or two people in the news each day and pray for them."

Lucille agreed. She felt better already. The next day Leonard suggested praying for an old woman being evicted from her apartment, and Lucille prayed for a man who was charged with grand theft. After only one day, they felt renewed as they began taking their petitions to God—the only one who can change the news from bad to good.

When you feel powerless over a situation in your life or in the world around you, take your concerns to God in prayer. God hears and answers.

Come back, O LORD.
Rescue me. Save me
because of your mercy!

PSALM 6:4 GOD'S WORD

Houseguest

*But I, by your great mercy, will come into your house; in
reverence will I bow down toward your holy temple.*

PSALM 5:7 NIV

Perhaps you enjoy opening your home to traveling friends and relatives. You've probably been the recipient of warm hospitality as well. There's nothing quite like a comfortable bed, a hot meal, a good shower, and great conversation after a few days on the road. What a blessing it is to enter a house where there are love, warmth, relaxation, and care.

Imagine God himself extending such an invitation to you—an invitation to park yourself on his doorstep, to set down your load, and to partake of the spiritual food and drink he has prepared for you. What more could you want? There is no better host than the Lord of heaven and earth, and the place to be is God's place—known for unending mercy and rest available to all who enter and reverence his holy name.

*God is the Master of hospitality. It is his pleasure
to swing wide the doorway to his house and to
welcome all who call upon him and enter.*

Inspiring Words FROM THE PSALMS

You who fear the LORD, praise Him;
all you descendants of Jacob, glorify
Him, and stand in awe of Him, all
you descendants of Israel.

PSALM 22:23 NASB

Bouncing Back

End the wickedness of the ungodly, but help all those who obey you. For you look deep within the mind and heart, O righteous God.

PSALM 7:9 NLT

Wilma Jean, a genteel, slow-speaking woman in her mid-fifties,  says she was raised to be spared any form of hardship. Whatever she wanted—from toys as a child to a car and jewelry as a teen—she received. Following the death of Wilma Jean's father, she received a generous inheritance. On a whim, she decided to purchase a $300,000 yacht, but the sale fell through before it closed. So Wilma Jean decided on a $500,000 condominium in a downtown high-rise instead.

"In a matter of moments, I escalated my expenditure by $200,000—without planning, thinking, or asking anyone's advice," she says. Wilma Jean admits her entire adult life has been a series of "nutty decisions to keep myself from growing up." But today she is seeing some positive changes due to prayer. "I realize that only God can help me bounce back," she says.

When people lose control, only God can help them bounce back and begin again. He is there to help anyone make a fresh start.

When I felt secure, I said,
"I will never be shaken."

PSALM 30:6 NIV

Forever Friend

*Turn to me and have mercy on me, for I am
alone and in deep distress. My problems go
from bad to worse. Oh, save me from them all!*

PSALM 25:16–17 NLT

Many people feel a deep sense of loneliness even though they have
friends, neighbors, and family. They feel dis-
connected from others, unnoticed, and perhaps even neglected.

Friends may suggest they get involved in a
pastime like rowing or singing in a choral
group, or take up a team sport such as soft-
ball so they won't be alone. But it is a mistake
to confuse being alone with being lonely; they
are not the same. One can feel lonely in a crowd or live alone and
feel content.

*No one needs to be alone or lonely, however, as
long as God is there. He will honor and console
you if you turn your heart to him and ask for his
company. He will be the forever friend you may
have looked for all your life. Invite God to be your
forever friend. Once he is your primary relationship
and you enjoy the pleasure of his company, you
will never be lonely—or alone—again.*

*G*od makes a home for the lonely.

PSALM 68:6 NASB

First Things First

He does what's best for those who fear him—hears
them call out, and saves them. GOD sticks by all
who love him, but it's all over for those who don't.

PSALM 145:19–20 THE MESSAGE

I become exasperated with erratic drivers and the way my cowork-
er talks about her husband," Carol said. "But when I'm alone and
think about these people calmly, then I'm
more understanding. Maybe that speeding
driver is rushing to a hospital to visit a
dying relative. Maybe the person at work
just had a fight with her husband. I
shouldn't let my point of view stop
me from being a good friend or a
compassionate stranger to someone
who's hurting."

Carol said she also wants to be more responsive to those close to
her—like her father, who is in a nursing home, or her sister, who has
never married but always hoped for a husband. "I try to imagine how
God would respond. He'd probably speak softly to each one, reach
out and hug these people and say, 'I love you.' That's my goal."

Life is more satisfying and people feel better
about themselves when they show love rather
than judge, when they care instead of criticize.

The LORD says, "I will rescue those who love me. I will protect those who trust in my name."

PSALM 91:14 NLT

Heart Talks

*The LORD looks from heaven; He sees all the sons of
men. From the place of His dwelling He looks
on all the inhabitants of the earth; He fashions their
hearts individually; He considers all their works.*

PSALM 33:13–15 NKJV

Parents are busy working. Kids are up to their chins with homework, sports, and music lessons. Most families have such full sched-

ules it's a challenge to find time to talk and relax together. Jon, father of five, has found a way. He says some of the best talks with his kids occur when they're in the car running errands or while doing chores on Saturday morning. "We have great family times," he said, "but it's also important to be with my kids one-on-one. When we're alone they open up." Even a thirty-minute outing seems like a major event to a child, yet it's a small investment for the parent.

If you feel pressed for time and torn between the responsibilities at work and those at home, consider introducing heart talks. They can occur anytime, anywhere a dad or mom and a child are together just being themselves.

*Heart talks between parents and children are a
great way to get to know more about one
another and to build family intimacy.*

Rejoice in the LORD and be glad,
you righteous; sing, all you who
are upright in heart!

PSALM 32:11 NIV

Special Instructions

He casts forth His ice as fragments; who can stand before
His cold? He sends forth His word and melts them; He
causes His wind to blow and the waters to flow.

PSALM 147:17–18 NASB

God has plenty to say to his people—all they have to do is listen. The Bible holds God's instructions for almost every area of life. In the Psalms, the writer passes on God's words of comfort, guidance, and practical wisdom, and the psalmist states that God is the one above all who deserves your praise, worship, and obedience.

The psalmist also reminds you that God delights in you and that even when you stumble, you won't fall because God will be there to catch you. God delivers faithful people from the wicked and is their stronghold, their King, and their companion.

If you are in a low spot in life, turn to God's Word.
You can cast all your cares on him and he will
sustain you. He will not disappoint you. No one
needs to be alone in the world, confused about
what to do in life. God's instructions to his people
are always available through prayer and the Bible.

I bow down toward your holy temple and give thanks to your name for your steadfast love and your faithfulness, for you have exalted above all things your name and your word.

PSALM 138:2 ESV

New Life from the Ashes

I will walk at liberty, for I seek Your precepts.
I will also speak of Your testimonies before
kings and shall not be ashamed.

PSALM 119:45–46 NASB

Zach and his wife, Marta, survived a fire that swept through their community in Southern California. Their house was the only one left standing on a street where forty homes once stood. "We're humbled and grateful for this new lease on life," said Zach. "It feels like we've been given a second chance—maybe for a purpose we don't know about yet."

In the midst of the charred remains, however, good abounded. People rushed to one another's aid. Food, clothing, shelter, and transportation poured into the city. Men and women who didn't know one another before the blaze became like family. They laughed and cried together, made plans to rebuild, to share potluck meals, to pool their clothing, and to give away what they could spare.

"I want everyone to know there is a God who loves us, who'll walk us through even the toughest times," Marta said as she stood next to the back fence and watched the sun rise over the blackened hills.

God will never leave or forsake those who look to him for guidance. He will bring forth new life even from the ashes.

I run to you, GOD; I run for
dear life. Don't let me down!
Take me seriously this time!

PSALM 31:1 THE MESSAGE

After All These Years

*This is the day the LORD has made. We will rejoice
and be glad in it. Please, LORD, please save us.
Please, LORD, please give us success.*
PSALM 118:24-25 NLT

"Mom, I got the job," Kristine shouted into the phone. "I start work next Monday," she added, waving the letter of acceptance from the manager of one of Chicago's fine restaurants. Kristine had finally realized her dream of becoming a professional chef.

"I'm so happy for you, Kristine. I knew you'd make it. You've been cooking since you were a child. Now you'll get paid for it!" How about you? What is your dream? Do you want to be an accomplished musician? Own your own landscaping business? Become a respected surgeon or teacher or politician? Sometimes all that is required to get started is being willing and then doing a bit of homework to discover the steps necessary to move forward.

*God will show you the way if you ask him. He
wants to bless you with success and prosperity.
True success comes from the hand of God when
you use the talents he gave you to honor him and
to contribute to the world around you.*

When you shall eat of the fruit of
your hands, you will be happy
and it will be well with you.

PSALM 128:2 NASB

Time-Out

Be at rest once more, O my soul, for the LORD has been
good to you. For you, O LORD, have delivered my soul
from death, my eyes from tears, my feet from stumbling.
PSALM 116:7–8 NIV

*I*f you're a sports fan, you're familiar with the time-out, when players huddle for instructions or move to the bench to catch their breath. Life is a lot like baseball, football, or hockey in that regard. You play hard and fast, but there comes a time when you need a break, an opportunity to pass the hours free of obligation. Perhaps your idea of a time-out is a weekend at the beach curled up in front of a fire with a good book.

Everyone needs a time-out. God wants it for you too. He calls you away from the daily grind to a period of silence and serenity where you can see and hear with new eyes and ears, where you can filter out the rhetoric of the world and instead tune in to the peace of God.

Every human being needs some R and R in order to
maintain good health and a balanced life.
Time-outs are also part of God's plan for your life.

He who dwells in the shelter of the Most High will abide in the shadow of the Almighty. I will say to the LORD, "My refuge and my fortress, my God, in whom I trust."

PSALM 91:1–2 ESV

Honest Abe

You will show me the way of life,
granting me the joy of your presence
and the pleasures of living with you forever.
PSALM 16:11 NLT

On Palm Sunday in 1865, men and women practically danced in the streets. The Civil War was over. President Lincoln thanked God

for the victory, then turned the attention of the nation to the long task of restructuring and healing the South so the country could be unified once again.

Just five days later, on the Friday before Easter, a different sound was heard in the streets—the sound of mourning over the news that President Lincoln had died following a fatal gunshot wound while watching a play at the Ford Theater in Washington, D.C. Even before he was laid to rest, people began referring to him as the "savior of the nation." Honest Abe, however, would have been uncomfortable to be elevated to such a height. And yet God had used Abraham Lincoln, a humble and obedient servant, at a particular time in United States history.

God often uses ordinary men and women to fulfill his eternal purposes. Those whom he chooses he equips for the appointed time.

Keep me as the apple of
your eye; hide me in the
shadow of your wings.

PSALM 17:8 NIV

A Stone's Throw

*Their plowmen plowed long furrows up and
down my back; then GOD ripped the
harnesses of the evil plowmen to shreds.*
PSALM 129:3–4 THE MESSAGE

Ten women stood on a hill overlooking Dorothy Lake in the
Sierra Mountains, each holding a handful of
stones. Their hiking leader had suggested they take
a few moments before ending the trip to think
about what situations and feelings they wanted to
leave behind so they could return home refreshed
and renewed.

"Pick up a few stones," she said, "and assign
to each one a feeling, event, or relationship that's
keeping you stuck. Say good-bye to each one, then pitch them."
Soon the women were throwing stones, one after another, with all
their might. Then the group erupted in laughter. Everyone admitted
feeling lighter, freer, ready to return home with a new perspective.

*Are there stones in your life weighing you down? An
exercise such as throwing stones can be physically and
emotionally freeing for a time, but for lasting freedom
from the past, release your stones to God in prayer.
True freedom from one's past comes from God alone
when you turn to him in submission and humility.*

*B*ring my soul out of prison, so that I may give thanks to Your name; the righteous will surround me, for You will deal bountifully with me.

PSALM 142:7 NASB

Heavenly Wonders

I look up at your macro-skies, dark and enormous,
your handmade sky-jewelry, moon and stars
mounted in their settings. Then I look at my micro-
self and wonder, Why do you bother with us?

PSALM 8:3–4 THE MESSAGE

Thirteen-year-old Jeremy and his mother, Joan, walked out into the yard at 3:00 in the morning and took position behind their telescope, eager to watch an array of shooting stars, and to locate various constellations in the clear night sky.

"It was one of the most precious moments I've ever had with my son," said Joan. "It was also a spiritual moment. I felt so small when I looked up and thought of the God of all creation. If he can keep the stars and the moon and the planets in their place, surely he can keep me."

Do you focus so much on what's in front of you that
you forget to look up? Many people do. But when
you view yourself as just one part of the great
cosmos, you're more likely to see how great God is to
have included you in his plan and purpose. Though
you are only one small part of God's great universe,
he loves you and has a purpose for your life.

O Jehovah, our Lord, the majesty and glory of your name fills the earth.

PSALM 8:9 TLB

Hang On

*LORD, you know the hopes of the helpless. Surely you will listen to
their cries and comfort them. You will bring justice to the orphans
and the oppressed, so people can no longer terrify them.*

PSALM 10:17–18 NLT

Samson, one of Israel's judges featured in the Old Testament, was
anything but an exemplary man. As a
teenager he rebelled against his mother's
teaching, broke nearly all of God's laws,
and hid his actions from his parents. His
mother probably questioned herself, won-
dering if there was something more she
could have done to guide her son to live an
upright life before God.

She succeeded in motivating him to look the part of a holy man.
He did not drink wine or cut his hair. Beneath the surface, something
was missing—a close relationship with God, the only one who could
provide the power and guidance he needed. Though Samson ruled
for twenty years, eventually lust got the best of him. Before he died
at an early age, he repented and returned to God.

*A rebellious teenager becomes an arrogant adult,
separating himself from others and from God. But
God is merciful to those who finally turn from
their transgressions and seek repentance.*

Reveal your miraculous deeds of mercy, O Savior of those who find refuge by your side from those who attack them.

PSALM 17:7 GOD'S WORD

Safe in God's Arms

He delivered me from my strong enemy, and from those who hated me, for they were too mighty for me. They confronted me in the day of my calamity, but the LORD was my stay.

PSALM 18:17–18 NASB

Thomas "Stonewall" Jackson was a man of immense courage on the battlefield and off. He graduated from West Point after nearly being turned away, and he later fought with distinction in the Mexican War. In 1861 he joined the Confederate army and fought in the Battle of Bull Run. There he earned his famous nickname as his brigade stood "like a stone wall" before a Union attack. Jackson was convinced that the South's cause was God's cause, and he remained firm.

When asked early in his military career how he could remain calm when a storm of shells and bullets rained down, he said without hesitation, "My religious beliefs teach me to feel as safe in battle as in bed. God has fixed the time for my death." Jackson lived his life ready for that day whenever it came.

God knows the hour of your birth and of your death. With that certainty you can live your life without fear, making the most of the time you have been given.

You called in trouble,
and I delivered you.

PSALM 81:7 NKJV

Invisible Protection

You give me your shield of victory,
and your right hand sustains me;
you stoop down to make me great.

PSALM 18:35 NIV

Nehemiah was an Israelite who worked for King Artaxerxes of
Persia. During a visit with his brother from Judah, Nehemiah asked

about the condition of Jerusalem and the
Jewish people.

His brother reported that the city's
wall was down and the people were in
great trouble, open to attack. Nehemiah
was disturbed by the news and wanted to
help repair the wall as well as the spirit of
the people. But he knew he couldn't simply leave the king. So he
prayed for an opportunity to approach the king. God answered his
prayer one day while Nehemiah was serving wine. When the king
asked why he looked sad, Nehemiah described the situation. The
king allowed him to go and help. Later Nehemiah reported that
"because the gracious hand of my God was upon me, the king granted my requests (Nehemiah 2:8 NIV)."

Prayer is the best first step before making an
important decision or request. God will provide a
way to realize your goal if it is in accord with his will.

The LORD is my strength and my shield; in him my heart trusts, and I am helped; my heart exults, and with my song I give thanks to him.

PSALM 28:7 ESV

What You Need

You send forth Your Spirit, they are created;
and You renew the face of the ground.
PSALM 104:30 NASB

There was a master artist who produced the most beautiful stained-glass windows anyone had ever seen. One of his students  observed him work, and then he decided he couldn't create the beauty his master did because he did not have the same kind of tools. He asked the master if he could borrow his tools, and the request was granted. For several weeks he toiled, attempting to create something of great beauty. But instead, his work looked like it always had.

One day, a colleague of the master artist was in the studio watching the student work. The student told the visitor he could not produce windows of great beauty even though he was using the master's tools. The wise visitor said to him, "Son, it is not the tools of the master you need. It is the spirit of the master."

Similarly, God's Spirit is what you need. The
holy hookup defeats the human inadequacy.
God's Spirit makes the difference.

I have seen you in the sanctuary
and beheld your power and your
glory. Because your love is better
than life, my lips will glorify you.

PSALM 63:2–3 NIV

Inspiring Words
SERIES

This and other books in the Inspiring Words series are available from your local bookstore.

Inspiring Words from the Psalms

Inspiring Words from the Psalms for Mothers

Inspiring Words from the Psalms for Women

Inspiring Words from the Psalms for Friends

Blue Sky Ink
Brentwood, Tennessee